C000164502

# EMBRACING YOURSELF WITH SELF-COMPASSION

*Stop Being Your Own Antagonist, Take a Deep Look at Yourself, Let Go of The Past Mistakes, Embrace a Positive Beginning and Learn The Peace of Self-Acceptance*

# Table of Contents

# Introduction

Fostering a sense of self-compassion and self-acceptance can be challenging even for a healthy and well-rounded adult. Despite how important these two characteristics are, very few people are taught about how to utilize them in their personal lives. Instead, we are often taught to be hard on ourselves, push ourselves as far as we can, and demand the maximum results out of our efforts. While challenging yourself to achieve substantial growth is valuable, pushing yourself to the point where it becomes self-sabotaging is not a positive habit to support.

If you truly want to achieve all of the success that you desire in life, you need to have a clear understanding of your mental wellbeing and around how you can support it so that you can improve your chances of succeeding. Without a strong mindset to back them up, most people will fail to achieve their desired level of success because despite having the best of intentions, they will struggle to keep themselves focused and motivated. Through the emotional and mental self-sabotaging behaviors such as having an overly harsh inner critic or trying to push through challenging emotions without acknowledging their purpose or healing them, they will simply burn out and fail to thrive.

As you listen through this audiobook, realize that you are going to be granted every single tool you need to begin developing the skills to become more self-compassionate and self-accepting. From identifying how to feel your emotions and develop a relationship to building a productive mindfulness and self-awareness practice, everything is devoted to helping you motivate yourself in a healthy way. The tools in this audiobook will not encourage or motivate you to become complacent, lose focus, or stop aiming for your dreams with any less intensity than you already have been. Instead, they will support you in having a stronger focus on how you can achieve your goals without compromising your inner sense of wellbeing. As a result, all of the success that you earn in your life will feel far more meaningful and positive.

If self-compassion has been particularly challenging for you until now, or if the concept itself seems foreign, I encourage you to really set the intention to approach this audiobook and the subjects within it with an open mind. You will get the most out of each chapter and all of the tools provided if you give yourself permission to see things from a new perspective at least for the duration of this audiobook. Fully embrace the practice of not only learning about and understanding these concepts and tools but actually working towards putting them into practice in your life as well. As you begin to see just how powerful they are and how they support you in moving forward towards a more positive future, you will quickly begin to realize why they matter so much.

Lastly, there is one major concept that you need to realize before you begin listening this audiobook. That is — self-compassion is an act of self-care, but it is also a tool that is learned through personal development practices. You are not going to be able to achieve self-compassion all in one attempt, nor will you truly be able to measure or grade yourself on the level of self-compassion that you currently have or that you develop. While there are ways for you to track your improvements and we will go into detail on those ways later, you need to understand that this practice is solely about helping yourself feel better and feel more positive in your approach to life. By allowing yourself to embody that balance, you will begin to feel far more peaceful overall.

Now, if you are ready to embark on the next chapter of your journey in self-development, it is time that you begin! Remember, self-compassion is a powerful tool for you to equip yourself with, so approach this audiobook as open-mindedly as you possibly can. And of course, enjoy the process!

# Chapter 1: Understanding the Self

Your Self or your identity is an important element of who you are. When you consider who you are, the illusion that you come up with is how you identify yourself. Although we tend to believe that our selves are an inherent part of who we are and that our personal beliefs over ourselves are finite and final, the reality is that who we are and who we think we are, typically reflect two entirely different people. Many people fail to realize that there is a difference and often find themselves genuinely believing that they are the person whom they envision in their minds and that there is no other alternative or option. As a result, they may end up developing a highly toxic, unrealistic, and self-sabotaging image or belief around who they are.

Realizing that who you truly are and who you think you are is two different people can come as a sense of relief to many. When you discover that there is a good chance that you do not actually align with the images or beliefs you have created, you realize that there is an opportunity for you to see yourself in a new light. You may even get the opportunity to start seeing yourself more clearly for who you really are, rather than for the illusion that you have been holding onto in your mind. In fact, by detaching from the strict identity you have held onto in your mind, you can give yourself the opportunity to begin experiencing far more compassion towards yourself in your life.

Identity is a rather complex topic that extends far beyond the image we carry of ourselves and the image that other's carry. In fact, there is an entire psychological study devoted to understanding identity and your sense of self and helping you discover exactly "who" you are. This field of study is known as social science and is comprised of psychologists and researchers who are actively seeking to understand identity to an even deeper level and get a clear sense of what makes a person's identity. Because there are so many different levels of identity, the study itself is quite expansive and continues to discover what one's true identity is versus the way they identify themselves and the way others identify them. In the following sections, you are going to get a deeper insight into what your sense of self truly is, how it is made up, and how your sense of self impacts the way you live your life.

## Discovering the Multiple Selves

There are two ways that people have multiple sense of self. The first way that you can experience multiple senses of self comes from how you interact with the people around you and the identity you possess around these people. For example, the self you are around your friends is likely quite different from the self you are around your family or your co-workers. Your environment is a huge factor in which role you will play, depending on where you are and who you are actively surrounded by. The second way that you experience multiple social selves is determined between the way you perceive yourself and the way others perceive you. Since everyone has had their own unique interactions and experiences with you, it is not unreasonable to realize that everyone sees you slightly different from how others see you. For example, your best friend may see you completely different from how your other friends may see you, or your Grandma may carry a completely different belief of who you are compared to the rest of the world. The relationship that people share with you, the experiences that you share together, and their perception of you and of people in general will all impact how people identify you. As a result, you actually have multiple identities – and no, that does not mean that you are having an identity crisis or that you have something wrong with you. It is actually entirely normal to have many identities.

When it comes to identifying yourself, you must realize that on a psychological front, you are not identifying yourself as one person inhabiting one body. You are identifying yourself based on the actual identity that you carry or the characteristics and personality traits that you are perceived to have. Your "self" is the conscious aspect of you that interacts with the world around you, communicates with other people, and shares experiences with others. Although there is no scientific evidence that proves that there is an out-of-body "self," most psychologists believe that the self is not attached to or identified by a person's body. Instead, it is the dimension of you that exists in your mind or the aspects of you that make up "who" you are beyond your physical and biological self.

This part of yourself that is not defined by your body or biology is typically described in three related but separable domains when it comes to psychological understanding. This means that there are three elements that coincide to make up your "self" or your identity. The first domain is known as your experiential self which is also known as the 'theatre of consciousness.' This part of yourself is identified as your first-person sense of being or how you personally experience the world around you. This part of yourself remains consistent over periods of time which results in psychologists believing that it is very closely linked to your memory. The second part of your identity is what is known as your private self-consciousness. This is your inner narrator or the voice that verbally narrates what is happening in your life to you privately within your mind. When you are reading, learning, or interpreting the world around you, this voice is actively narrating how you are interpreting that information and what sense you are making of it. This is the part of you that carries your beliefs and values about how the world works. Neuroscientist Antonio Damasio calls your private self-consciousness your autobiographical self because it is regularly narrating your autobiography in your mind. The third and final dimension of your identity is your public self or your persona. This is the image that you attempt to project to others through your actions, attitudes, behaviors, and words. This is the part of your self that other people interact with and see which results in this being the part of yourself that people generate perceptions around. It is through your persona that people determine what your identity is according to them and their own understanding.

With all that being said, the multiple selves that you embody comes from the persona that you share with others. People will then generate perceptions around who you are, what your identity is, and how they feel about that. It is through this persona that people will decide if they can relate to you, if they like you, and anything else relating to how they feel about you. In realizing that people generate their perceptions of you based off of one single aspect of who you truly are, it helps you realize that their perspective is not accurate. In fact, neither is yours. No one, including yourself, *truly* knows who you actually are. Everything is just generated based on beliefs, values, perspectives, and understandings that have been accumulated through varying life experiences.

## Relationship with Ourselves

The relationship that you share with yourself often develops somewhere between the first and second dimensions of your identity. The way you interpret and interact with the world around you, combined with your beliefs and values helps you generate a sort of self-awareness that allows you to begin determining what you believe your identity is. Again, just like with other people, your identity is largely based off of your perception and understanding of the world around you and how it works. Even if your own perception is rarely accurate when compared to who you actually are which is a unique blend of all three layers of your dimensional identity.

Because your relationship with yourself is largely defined by your beliefs and values and your ability to live in alignment with them or not, it is easy to realize that how you identify yourself can be easily shifted based on your perceptions. If you carry certain core beliefs about how people should live, for example, and you are not living in alignment with those beliefs, then you may generate a perception that identifies you as someone who is bad or unworthy. You might relate yourself to the identities you have mentally designed for other people in society who you believe to be bad too which can result in you seeing yourself in an extremely negative light. If you carry certain core beliefs about how people should live and you *are* living in alignment with them, you may praise yourself and see yourself as good and special. You might then find yourself relating more to people in society who you see as good and positive, thus allowing you to cast yourself in a positive light.

The reality is that none of us are truly inherently good or bad, we are all just perceiving, experiencing, and responding to the world around us. Generating internal images of what is positive and what is not only results in you setting standards for yourself on how you should behave. If these standards are beyond what you can reasonably achieve or do not align with what you genuinely want in life, then you may find yourself adhering to beliefs and values that are actually rather destructive. Instead of helping you live a life of contentment and satisfaction, you may find these beliefs leading to you constantly feeling incapable and under confident. As a result, your relationship with yourself may deteriorate because the way in which you view yourself is not reasonable or compassionate.

## Everyone Has Their Own Filters and Explanatory Styles

To help you develop your understanding of how your perception of yourself varies from other's perception of you, let's discuss personal filters and explanatory styles. Understanding why everyone has such different views of the world allows you to have a stronger understanding as to why there are so many aspects of your identity based on your own personas and the way that people perceive them and you. The concept of personal filters and explanatory styles is simple. A personal filter is how you see the world and your explanatory style is how you explain it to yourself and to others.

Every single person has a unique filter and explanatory style that is based on their own unique experiences in life. All of the interactions they have had, the situations they have encountered, and things they have been told by the people around them shape the way that they view life itself. How each of these small yet impactful things come together will shape how each person perceives the world around them, others that cohabit the planet with them, and themselves. So, for example, if someone along the way has learned that not washing your dishes every day is a sign of laziness and ignorance, then that person is going to believe that anyone who leaves dishes in the sink overnight is somehow "bad," including themselves.

The foundation of a person's filters and explanatory styles are rooted in childhood when a child is not yet able to generate their own independent thoughts and beliefs. Until we are six years old, our ability to critically think about things and generate our own opinions independent of the opinions of others is virtually non-existent so we absorb everything we learn. This means that anything your parents said, people around you were saying, or you were shown through other's behaviors and actions were anchored into your mind as the foundation of your personal beliefs and values. Even though you gained the capacity to think critically and start generating your own opinions around six years old, you were still actively internalizing what everyone told you because, in most cases, no one ever taught you otherwise. As a result, you likely have many different beliefs and values that stemmed in your childhood which have gone on to impact you for years to come. In fact, these very beliefs and values are believed to make up a lot of what your autobiographical-self narrates to yourself on a daily basis, thus shaping the way you see yourself. See, who you think you are may not even be an accurate reflection of how *you* think, it may actually be an internalization based on the beliefs and values you were taught by people as you were growing up.

Since every single person will hear different things throughout their lives even if they are raised in similar environments, the way that every person views and interprets the world around them varies. Even siblings will grow up to have different perceptions and beliefs based on the way that they have internalized the beliefs they heard and were shown throughout their lifetimes. It is through this process that each person develops their own personal filters and explanatory styles for how they interpret and explain the world around them. Because of this, we can conclude that any beliefs that you have around who you are and any beliefs that others have around who you are do not actually define who you truly are. Instead, they define the belief systems that you have established throughout your life until this point.

When you realize that your beliefs are what shape your *perception* of your identity and not your identity itself, it becomes a lot easier for you to have compassion for yourself. You begin to realize that how you see yourself is not necessarily a true reflection of who you are, but instead a way that you have been lead to view yourself. This view was designed to support you in feeling connected to your 'tribe' or family and community, but in some cases, it can become destructive and result in you feeling deeply disconnected from yourself. When that happens, realizing that you are not inherently 'bad' or 'wrong' because you do not feel like you fit in makes it a lot easier for you to have compassion for your feelings and for the experiences you are going through. As a result, healing from these painful emotions and moving forward into a more self-compassionate and self-loving future becomes a lot easier for you.

## Your Environment and Your Values

We have already discussed the nature of values but you may be wondering where *exactly* your values come from and why you develop them in the first place. In "The Four Agreements" by author Don Miguel Ruiz describes humans as being self-domesticated creatures. His take on it is that we learned how to organize ourselves into societies and develop basic rules and regulations for those societies. These rules are designed to keep us safe and help us all work together to contribute to the greater good of society without the vicious outbursts of quarreling or fighting to the death like we often see happening in other species. In order for us to adhere to these rules and continue working together as a society and not be punished by society for breaking those rules, we develop values. These values help us determine what is right and what is wrong so that we can navigate domesticated living and continue being accepted by and welcomed into our society. When we act 'right', we are appreciated, loved, and nurtured. When we act 'wrong', we are punished, shunned, and outcast by our loved ones or our community.

Rules and values are generally a very positive thing that helps us to maintain a positive society that continues to operate effectively and productively. When it comes to looking at our communities as a whole, these support us in determining how we can all cohabit our cities, provinces or states, countries, and continents in a way that is consistent and agreed upon. Although not every locality is governed in the same way, the way that each locality is governed is agreed upon and is accepted by other governed localities. That way, everyone is able to coexist without having to experience the worry of being harmed by anyone else in the community and if it does happen, the person who committed the harming will be penalized for their actions.

Of course, society has its flaws and not everyone is held accountable for their actions, but the general structure works towards keeping everyone together and keeping our societies 'civilized' and functional. Unfortunately, the structure ends up falling down into cliques or areas of society where the specific values and beliefs are more strict and specific than the general society. In a standard society, the values and rules are generally simple. Typically, they involve things like do not harm others and obey the laws so that everyone cooperates in a uniformed way that minimizes the harms to others and keeps the society functioning and moving forward. In subsections of society such as within different cultures, religions, neighborhoods, or even within families and social circles, different values often arise. Typically, these values are a lot more specific and restrictive than the overall values of any given society. These also tend to be the values that we adopt throughout our lifetimes and are the foundation upon which we decide everything including right from wrong. Through these more restrictive values, we are typically lead to walk a very specific path in order to keep us being accepted and loved by our social circles. We learn these values through our parents' parenting styles, the words of our friends, and the harsh words of bullies. As we listen to the people close to us communicate, gossip, and either praise or reprimand each other for their behaviors, we develop an inner system of values. These values are meant to help us fit in, not only with society as a whole but with our subsection of society within which we were raised. This is how we are able to stay close and connected with the people that we care about and accepted into our personal 'tribes.'

Where our environment can begin to become toxic is when it supports us in developing values that do not actually match our personal beliefs and opinions. For example, say you are raised in a community that believes in Christian and Christian teachings, but you personally feel a deeper connection with Buddhism and Buddhist teachings. In this scenario, the values that you have learned throughout your life may prevent you from pursuing your desired life path because you fear that you will be shunned or punished by your loved ones. Although you would not be reprimanded by society as a whole, you would likely experience friction with the people you are closest with which could make it feel as though you are being completely abandoned or separated from your 'herd' or group. The fear of being separated results in you feeling the same sensations that a wild animal may feel if they were separated from their own herd — anxious, fearful, stressed out and worried about their ability to survive. Of course, choosing to go your own way in a civilized society will likely not result in overly negative or life-threatening repercussions but it is definitely a stressful experience.

The very fear of being shunned leads many people to find themselves accepting and living by values that are not their own so that they can avoid having to be isolated from their group. As they continue to adhere to the values they do not personally believe in, the person will continue to generate feelings of 'I am bad' or 'I am wrong.' These feelings will continue to grow as long as the values a person is accepting and living by are not in alignment with the beliefs that they genuinely have inside. You may understand exactly what this feels like if you are currently living in a state where the values that you are attempting to live by do not accurately reflect how you feel about life itself.

## Discover and Understand Your Emotions

Although values can be powerful in helping societies grow together and stay functional, they can also lead to deep inner struggles with varying thoughts and challenging emotions. This is especially true for people living in an environment that does not accurately reflect their personal values and beliefs. The more you live out of alignment with your personal values, the more your autobiographical voice will become plagued with negative thoughts that bully you. The words you have heard from your own bullies or as others were gossiping about people who were not deemed "acceptable" by your group will ring through your mind. Each time you behave or think in a way that you know would be considered bad or wrong by your group, you will play out thoughts in your mind such as 'Why can't I just be normal?' 'Why am I so bad at everything?' or 'Why can I never get it right?' As these thoughts continue playing out, you will find yourself feeling a deteriorating sense of self-esteem and self-confidence. Your ability to feel worthy and capable will diminish as you continually hold yourself up to standards that do not accurately reflect what you value or believe. In order to step out of the traps of these negative values and belief systems, you have to begin exploring the emotions that are keeping you trapped. You need to begin paying attention to how you are feeling, what your different thoughts are bringing up for you, and how your emotions are impacting your life. By assessing your overall

15

emotional state and getting really clear on what you are actually feeling inside, you can begin to discover whether or not you are actively living in alignment with your *true* values. If you are not, you will need to begin making changes so that you can start living a life that feels more aligned for you, which we will get deeper into later on.

In the meantime, recognizing your ongoing emotional state will give you a general idea as to whether or not your current sense of self is accurate and productive or inaccurate and destructive. If you are living in a chronic state of emotional turmoil and consistently feeling overwhelmed, worthless, unmotivated, or plagued by low self-esteem and low self-confidence, you can pretty much guarantee that your perception of your identity is flawed. It is likely that you are presently struggling to meet your personal values so your autobiographical self continues to attempt to help you 'fit in' to an identity that you do not actually fit into. As a result, each time you act out of alignment with that identity, your autobiographical self reprimands you the same way that people in your group or society would reprimand you if they knew what you were doing or thinking. Although the function of this aspect of yourself is designed to help you fit in and stay protected, it can also become highly damaging and create intense feelings of self-loathing and unworthiness. For that reason, it is important that you identify if and when it is acting out of your best interest so that you can take back control and begin acting in deeper alignment with who you *really* are.

If your emotions are generally positive or content but you find yourself occasionally feeling intense bursts of emotional turmoil, chances are you are living in alignment with your core values for the most part. However, there are likely specific times in your life where your personal values and the external values (or the values of those around you) are not in alignment. As a result, you may find yourself feeling angry, sad, or fearful because you worry that if you do not meet the values of the other person, you will not be 'accepted.' In this case, you may not need to make as drastic of changes, but you will still need to take control over your mind, your inner beliefs, and your chosen behaviors to ensure that you are staying true to your inner self.

The best way to discover and understand your emotions is to begin journaling on a regular basis. Writing down your thoughts, feelings, and experiences when you have a particularly intense emotional response to the world around you or reflecting on them at the end of each day gives you the opportunity to identify what you are actually feeling. As you journal, seek to accurately reflect everything that you are truly feeling by getting to the root of those emotions and identifying them by their true name. So, if you are feeling a sense of jealousy towards someone because they seem to fit in better than you do, make sure that you label that emotion as jealousy and not as something like anger or frustration. That way, you can honestly understand what it is that you are feeling and give that emotion the acknowledgment that it craves. You can also then look into identifying *why* you are feeling that emotion by writing down what beliefs or values you have that lead to that emotion coming up in the first place. If you are unsure, simply analyze your thoughts and see what they suggest. For example, if your thoughts were reflecting jealousy because you wanted to fit in and you felt like another person fit in with *ease*, then the belief that you have may be that fitting in with people should be easy. Because you were not experiencing ease in fitting in or you had to work so hard to defy your own personal values, you may then feel like you are bad or there is something wrong with you because it was not easy for you. In reality, it likely is easy for you to fit in, so long as you are hanging out with the right people who accurately reflect your values and beliefs. I recommend writing in this journal at least once per day so that you can begin getting a clearer understanding of your emotions, your values, and how your life may not be reflecting your values. As you begin to see this on paper, having compassion for yourself becomes a lot easier because you begin generating answers as to why you are not presently feeling like a person who is good or worthy.

## Explore Your Fears and Insecurities

As you write down your emotions in your journal, chances are you will begin to generate a lot of entries that revolve around feelings of fears and insecurities. Your fears may sound silly or nonsensical in the grand scheme of things but realize that the very fact that you are feeling them makes them valid and worthy of being acknowledged and healed.

The fears and insecurities that you document, particularly if you discover that you are living largely out of alignment with your values will likely sound something like this:

- "I am afraid that I am not worthy of love."
- "No one loves me because _____."
- "If I change _____ I will have no one left."
- "I do not deserve to have my own path or way of doing things."
- "If I make a change they will not accept me."
- "I will be bullied if I act my own way."
- "My decision to go my own way could lead to eternal damnation."
- "(Your religious leader/deity) will not accept me if I honor my own values."
- "I am not allowed to be different."
- "I might die completely alone if I make any changes."

Fears and insecurities around losing the things that you have and around being unloved or unworthy of receiving love in your life if you choose to live in alignment with your own values is common. Many people who are living deeply out of alignment with their sense of self continue to live that way because they worry that if they honor their own belief or values then they will lose everything. The idea of losing their loved ones, their rite to heaven or a positive afterlife (if you are religious,) their status, their home, their worthiness, or any other thing they value is enough to keep them trapped in values that do not actually serve them.

Often, these fears are developed in childhood and are never challenged or adjusted as a person grows up. Although these fears are rarely an accurate reflection of what would happen if you were to begin living in alignment with your own values, the fear still exists. Until you choose to challenge those fears and really get to the root of them and heal them, you will continue living in a state of fear and discomfort even if those fears are unfounded.

The best way to challenge your fears is to ask yourself one very simple question: "and then what?" In asking yourself this question, you allow yourself to continue playing out the scenario of what might happen if you follow your own values until you reach the point where you realize that it is unlikely that anything bad will happen.

# Chapter 2: Self-Compassion

In our modern society, we are taught to apply as much pressure to ourselves as possible to attempt to get further ahead in our success. We often hear of various resources that are available surrounding the topics of "how to grow faster" or "how to achieve your goals sooner." What we rarely hear, however, is how to be compassionate with ourselves when we are not moving at the hyperspeed that society tends to dupe us into believing that we are meant to achieve. As a result, very few people truly know how to experience self-compassion when they are in a rut, struggling to advance in life, or not moving at the rapid pace that society deems as being "acceptable."

When you are unable to be compassionate with yourself, you end up putting even more pressure on yourself to achieve things that are simply not achievable within your realm of existence at that moment. Instead of being compassionate with yourself, you find yourself applying even more pressure to try and "jump start" the next level of your success or your life when, in reality, all you are doing is making yourself feel even worse. Rather than feeling motivated and ready to get into action, you end up feeling a lack of motivation and a deep inner feeling of not being good enough or worthy enough to achieve the success that you desire. In reality, your inability to move forward has nothing to do with you not being good enough or worthy enough, but everything to do with you not being compassionate enough. What you really need to be doing is showing yourself compassion, taking the time to understand why you are struggling, and equipping yourself with the tools that you need to overcome your emotions and take the next steps in your life. Sometimes, the fastest way through a hard time is to slow down and simply be compassionate with your self.

## Buddhist Psychology on Self-Compassion

In Buddhism, there is a big emphasis on the importance of self-compassion and how it helps literally shift a person's mind. Buddhists often teach self-compassion through the art of meditation which is used to help people not only become more cognitively aware but also more emotionally aware of themselves. Through sitting in mindful meditation, Buddhists are able to begin bringing their emotions to the forefront of their lives and recognizing them for what they are. They may also be able to identify why that emotion exists and what message it has to offer the person engaging in the meditation. Through their Zen traditions, Buddhist teachers will educate people on the importance of self-acceptance and self-compassion. In their eyes, these two practices are essential in leading to the state of *shunyata* or emptiness.

In psychotherapy, many positive psychologists have begun researching the concepts of self-acceptance and self-compassion as well. Through studying actions like meditation and self-compassion, psychologists have discovered that one of the easiest ways to predict a person's mental wellbeing both in the present and in the future is to analyze their sense of self-acceptance. A person who accepts themselves is more likely to be compassionate towards themselves as well, meaning that they are less likely to strive to achieve standards of success that do not resonate with their true beliefs.

While self-acceptance and self-compassion have always been valued, psychologists are really starting to understand how these two states of mindfulness are really contributing to a person's overall well-being. By learning how to improve your ability to experience self-acceptance and self-compassion such as through Buddhist meditation, you are able to change your thoughts towards ones that are more positive and productive. As a result, you do not find yourself trapped in a chronic state of feeling disappointed in yourself and as though you are failing in life.

## Why Self-Compassion Matters

Self-compassion is one of the most effective mental tools that you could possibly equip yourself with. When it comes to allowing yourself the opportunity to truly move forward in life, self-compassion is a key that will change everything. When you lack self-compassion, seeing yourself as a positive, worthy, good enough, and lovable human being can be extremely challenging. A lack of self-compassion can lead to you constantly striving to do more and be more because you struggle to be compassionate towards yourself when you do not reach unreasonably high standards in your life. This lack of self-compassion can lead to an obsession to become perfect which, as you likely know, is never worth pursuing since perfect truly is not an achievable standard for living.

When you inevitably fail to become the perfect person — the perfect friend, the perfect child, the perfect spouse, the perfect parent, the perfect employee, or any other role you play in your life, you end up feeling immense sadness inside. This sadness leads to you wondering what is wrong with you and why you cannot accomplish the perfect standard that you have set up for yourself. Rather than recognizing that perfect is not achievable and seeing your standard for the unreasonable expectation that it is, you end up seeing yourself as being incapable and unworthy. This type of misconception can lead to deep and painful inner feelings that ultimately lead to you not feeling capable or worthy of moving forward in your life due to an all-or-nothing view.

When you equip yourself with self-compassion, you change your point of view so that you can recognize yourself as being a human who is only capable of achieving human things in your life. Rather than attempting to hold yourself to the unattainable standards of perfectionism, you start to hold yourself to more reasonable and realistic standards that allow you to truly make progress in life. If you find yourself making a mistake or struggling with something, rather than immediately thinking that there is something wrong with you, you can instead focus on being compassionate towards yourself for your experience. Through self-compassion, you slow down, recognize your true emotions, and work through them in a loving and gentle way so that you can fully feel them and move on from them. With your challenging emotions or setbacks completely worked through and set aside, you can easily begin moving forward towards your goals again. As a result, even though you may seem like you are progressing slowly, you are actually progressing faster because you are not hitting extreme levels of burnout and overwhelm along the way. You also stop holding yourself back from your all-or-nothing attitude that leaves you feeling unwilling to begin projects for fear of not being able to accomplish them with perfection.

## Benefits of Self Compassion

Self-compassion has many positive benefits that can help you achieve a better life overall. When you are compassionate towards yourself, you essentially give yourself the gentle kindness that you crave during those periods of challenge. Think of your inner emotions as a small child. When you have challenging situations that lead to feelings of not being good enough or capable enough, it is likely that your emotions are frazzled, too. Rather than feeling positive and hopeful, you likely feel fearful, angry, sad, and even embarrassed. As a small child when you felt this way, you would crave the attention of an adult who was more experienced with their emotions that would be able to comfort you and tell you that everything was going to be okay. Likewise, as an adult with challenging or festering emotions, you likely still crave that very same experience — to have someone sit with you, console you through your challenges, and let you know that everything is going to be okay. Of course, as adults, it is not exactly reasonable to believe that we are going to have someone in our lives who can offer that for us every single time we hit a challenge so we have to become that person for ourselves.

That is where the benefits of self-compassion come in. When you begin to become the compassionate, gentle, loving, and kind adult that your inner child needs, overcoming challenges in your life becomes a lot easier. Instead of attempting to whip yourself into submission through abusive acts such as bullying yourself or applying even more pressure to yourself, you instead sit with yourself and console yourself. Through that gentle act of compassion, that part of you that feels abandoned, wrong, shameful, or fearful is able to be consoled and healed. You begin to experience greater feelings of happiness and optimism and your spirit becomes more curious and adventurous. As you continue to show more compassion for yourself, your inner wisdom develops and you become more confident in your ability to have a positive impact on those around you. You experience feelings of hope and faith and your ability to make a dream and pursue that dream is improved because you become a self-starter with a purpose. Since you are no longer bullying yourself into a state of being too afraid to move or make a decision, you are able to open up and move forward with a more positive and optimistic vision of the world and how your life can look.

Becoming self-compassionate does not mean that you won't run into challenges or sometimes experience fear or uncertainty, but instead, it means that you will know how to nurture yourself through those experiences. Through this nurturing ability, you will be able to find a path forward that genuinely feels good and allows you to grow and move with ease. You will break through the chains of pessimism and self-criticism that have been holding you back and begin living with a greater sense of intention and intensity, thus allowing you to move through any challenge you may face with certainty.

# Misconceptions about Self-Compassion

The modern world sees things like self-compassion as weak, ineffective, and soft. We are often taught that if we slow down and have compassion for ourselves that we must not be capable enough of moving forward through anything we face. Instead of being encouraged to have self-compassion, we are encouraged to fight harder and continue forcing ourselves forward until we truly lack any energy or will to keep fighting. Because of this conditioning, so many people do not see self-compassion as a positive, uplifting act that can truly help you. Instead, they see self-compassion as a negative, weak trait that proves that you are incapable and that something is wrong with you. This could not be further from the truth.

When you are expressing compassion for yourself, you are not showing a sign of weakness or proving that you are incapable of moving through a challenging obstacle. In fact, you are showing that you are equipped with the exact level of emotional intelligence required to move through anything. People who are self-compassionate know that by being compassionate towards themselves through challenging experiences, they can move through them with greater ease and without lasting repercussions. Through fully working through their emotions and having compassion for themselves along the way, self-compassionate people actually have a far more sustainable coping method than anyone else.

Self-compassion is also not a long-term pity party where you sit around and feel sorry for yourself and the troubles that you are experiencing in your life. When you experience self-compassion, you are not tuning out the bad things or wallowing in how troublesome your life truly is. Instead, you are actually tuning into your true emotions, acknowledging them, and processing those emotions in a complete manner. Through this completed process you are able to move on from the feelings that have you feeling incapable or unworthy and let go of them in a more complete manner, meaning that they will not linger and cause further problems in the future. As a result, you are actually using a very productive and solution-focused approach to your emotions, not one that is allowing you to simply sit around and play the victim of your own emotions.

Another common misconception about self-compassion, especially within people who experience perfectionism, is that being self-compassionate will lead to complacency. If you think that by showing yourself compassion you will be giving yourself an excuse or a pass to avoid having to make any progress in your life, you are carrying a false belief around what self-compassion truly is. Self-compassion is not intended to keep you from achieving anything in your life, if you are using it in this way then you are not using self-compassion but instead, you are using excuses. True self-compassion is not about allowing yourself to do nothing and achieve nothing. It is about being honest and realistic about what you can achieve and recognizing that your personal speed through life is plenty fast enough. You are not required to keep up with some heinous belief that you should be moving any faster than what is reasonable with you — you are allowed to move at your own pace and that is certainly enough.

A big fear that people tend to have is that if they become self-compassionate then they are somehow becoming narcissistic. This is completely untrue. Self-compassion and narcissism are entirely separate qualities and through being self-compassionate you are certainly not at risk of becoming narcissistic. True narcissism comes from an inner belief that you need to be better than everyone else around you and that you will do, say, and think anything that is required in order for you to achieve success in your life. A true narcissist is not someone who seeks to improve themselves genuinely, but rather is someone who feels a deep need to be better than everyone else as a result of a psychological disorder that causes them to see the world in a very disillusioned way. If you are self-compassionate, you are not approaching life through delusion, but instead through a highly intentional desire to actually improve yourself and experience a better life. True self-compassion is not the act of trying to be better than everyone else, it is the act of trying to be better than the person you were the day before.

Another thing that self-compassion isn't is selfish. In many scenarios, people who are expressing self-compassion are told by others that they are being selfish and inconsiderate towards those around them. For example, say that you struggle to have a positive experience at family gatherings because you tend to be treated negatively by your family. Choosing not to attend large family gatherings as an act of self-compassion would not be selfish but instead would be a positive form of self-care and self-consideration. Even though your family may attempt to bully you into thinking that you are being selfish, the reality is that you are simply being compassionate towards yourself and your needs by admitting that you do not want to sit through a negative dinner.

Lastly, self-compassion and self-esteem are not the same things. In recent years, a movement that is known as the "self-esteem movement" has risen to the surface and encouraged people to increase their self-esteem. Oddly enough, following the introduction of the self-esteem movement, narcissism increased with what is known as the "narcissism epidemic." Self-esteem is a word that measures or refers to the amount of confidence that one has in their own abilities or their amount of self-respect. On the other hand, self-compassion is the act of having compassion towards one's self. Unrelated to confidence and self-respect, self-compassion is having a sympathetic concern towards the suffering or misfortunes of yourself or others. When you have compassion for yourself, your goal is not to increase your confidence or your self-respect but instead to increase the amount of sympathy you have towards yourself and your personal experiences.

## Balancing the Act of Generosity

The myth that self-compassion is selfish likely stems from the idea that people who are self-compassionate are not generous or do not give generously to others. Often times, this myth arises either from people who are no benefiting from another person in their life choosing to be self-compassionate. For example, say you have a friend who regularly asks favors of you to the point that you feel like anytime they call you, you know there is a high chance that they are only calling you to ask for a favor. In this instance, if you were to stop saying "yes" all of the time and start saying "no" because no felt like an act of self-compassion, such as if you didn't truly have the energy or the means to fulfill the favor, your friend might get angry. They may begin to feel that you are being selfish or that you are being unfair when, in reality, you are simply exercising self-compassion by not overpromising yourself to other people.

Just because you choose to be self-compassionate does not mean that you are not going to be generous anymore, it simply means that anytime you are being generous it will be an act of self-love, too. You will no longer agree or promise to do things when you truly want to say no because you recognize that it is not in your best interest when you do, so you will practice self-compassion. Because you are no longer agreeing to so many things that make you feel bad, you will not have a constant feeling of being overwhelmed by doing things that you do not want to do. As a result, the generosity that you give will be more genuine and sincere and it will not weigh you down or lead you to feel overwhelmed or under cared for. This means that you will likely be even more generous towards others, except that your giving will be more focused on doing things that also make you feel good or happy. Through this selective generosity, you will have more energy to share and give and both you and the person that you are giving to will feel positive from what you are both receiving.

In order for you to begin balancing the acts of self-compassion and generosity, you need to start identifying where your boundaries are around giving. If you have never considered this before, chances are that you are giving far more than you truly need to be. This over giving has likely lead to you feeling burnt out, used, unappreciated, or completely frustrated at least once in your life but likely many times. When you begin to address where you feel the worst during your acts of generosity, you can start setting boundaries around these acts of giving so that you no longer feel so depleted after giving to others. For example, maybe a family member constantly expects too much of you and it feels overwhelming for you to attempt to fulfill their demands. Instead of finding yourself trapped in that constant state of overwhelm and resentment, you can start setting a boundary around how much you are willing to give to that person. Maybe you will only give when you genuinely feel like you have the energy, resources, and desire to do so and in all other circumstances, you will say no. This boundary, when upheld, will ensure that you are not depleting yourself by attempting to give too much to the said family member. It will take time for you to identify your boundaries and truly uphold them but once you do, upholding your boundaries and expressing self-compassion in the act of generosity will become much easier for you. Through this act of self-compassion, you will find that giving is more heartfelt and sincere and that you do not feel obligated to give every single time someone asks for something from you.

## How to Develop Your Self-Compassion

In a society that fails to truly honor the importance of self-compassion and regularly advocates for the exact opposite, you might be wondering — *"how can I become more compassionate towards myself?"* This answer is completely reasonable and justified, especially if compassion is not something that you have been taught or shown very often in your life. Below, I have outlined three steps that you can begin practicing today in order to start showing yourself more compassion throughout your life.

### *Practicing Forgiveness towards Yourself*

If you truly want to experience the fullness of self-compassion, you need to start practicing forgiveness towards yourself. Punishing yourself for your mistakes and holding yourself in contempt for your failures will only result in you feeling even more terrified about the idea of moving forward in your life. You need to begin accepting that you are not perfect and that it is completely natural for you to experience shortcomings. Everyone has flaws and everyone goes through the process of having to accept themselves regardless of what flaws they may have had in their past, may have in their present, or may develop in their future. The reason why people value you and why you should value yourself has nothing to do with whether or not you are flawed but rather who you are as an overall person. If you genuinely lead your life with a sincere heart and a positive intention, chances are, you are a great person and you deserve to have your forgiveness surrounding the mistakes that you have made in your life no matter how big or small.

### *Fostering a Growth Mindset*

To have a growth mindset means to be willing to focus on areas in your life where you can improve. Many people have a mindset of being "stuck in their ways" or "unable to change even if they wanted to." This mindset is not helpful when it comes to learning how to be self-compassionate as it will prevent you from developing your inner wisdom which typically coincides with developing your self-compassion. By approaching life with a sense of curiosity and a willingness to grow, you not only open yourself up to the wisdom that you need to accept yourself but you also open yourself up to the mindset that you need to accept your shortcomings. A growth mindset means that you are focused on growth, not on perfection, so the idea of failing or making a mistake becomes a lot less scary because perfectionism is not your main goal, growth is. In order to begin shifting your mindset away from perfectionism and towards growth, start focusing on quieting the voice of your inner critic. Avoid comparing yourself to others no matter who they are and start looking for people who inspire you to become a better person. Having role models who also foster a growth mindset and who already have self-compassion or who are working towards it make fostering your own growth mindset far more achievable.

### *Expressing Gratitude*

Gratitude is a state of mind that leaves you feeling genuinely grateful for all of the blessings that you have in your life. When you are grateful, your ability to experience joy and abundance in your life is far superior to when you are not. You also teach yourself to start focusing on more positive things in life so that you can take your focus away from places like your flaws or your shortcomings. A great way to begin developing self-compassion specifically is to start expressing gratitude towards yourself on a daily basis. Each day, look in the mirror and express three to five reasons for why you are grateful for yourself. This could be anything from your willingness to continue learning and finding a way to feel better to your ability to cultivate new friendships and find a company anywhere you go. Try and choose new things every day so that you can start accumulating a list of reasons as to why you are such a great person and why you deserve to have your own sense of self-compassion.

# Chapter 3: Self-Acceptance

Self-acceptance is the next step in learning how to have self-compassion. When you develop a sense of self-acceptance, you become far more willing to accept yourself as you are. As a person who features self-acceptance, you allow yourself to become more aware of your strengths and weaknesses and to remain realistic about your talents and capabilities. You also generate a deeper sense of self-worth because you begin to realize that you, like everyone else, are inherently worthy and that there is nothing you have to do in order to earn your worthiness. In other words, none of your shortcomings, flaws, mistakes, or inabilities results in you becoming worthless or undeserving. You recognize that you possess a unique set of skills and characteristics that blend together to develop a person who is certainly worthy and deserving of having and experiencing good things in life.

In this chapter, you are going to discover what self-acceptance is, how it can be achieved, and what you need to do in order to begin having self-acceptance towards yourself. A great place to start is to begin right now by accepting yourself as you are, even if that means accepting the fact that you currently struggle to accept certain aspects of yourself or your life. By having an unconditional level of self-acceptance towards yourself, you open yourself up to the opportunity to be okay with who you are. When you are okay with who you are, having compassion towards yourself for who or what you are not or for the experiences that you have becomes far easier.

## The Myth of Perfection

In our childhoods, we are taught that we need to adhere to societal standards in order to be accepted, loved, appreciated, or praised by the people around us. We learn this by being celebrated and praised every time we do something great, ignored if we only do something good, or punished if we underperform. As a result, we are driven to start performing as great as we possibly can every single time we set out to accomplish something. What ends up happening is that our standards for the great increase each time as we realize that upon doing everything great so many times over, people stop praising us because they come to expect that level of greatness from us. For some people, not receiving continual praise from others is plenty because they have learned how to praise and celebrate themselves, so they simply continue achieving what feels like a high standard of greatness within themselves. For others, they crave that praise and celebration so deeply that they will continue to attempt to outperform themselves and achieve as close to perfect results as possible in order to receive positive attention. When they do not receive that positive attention, they take it as a sign that they are not doing well enough and that they need to do even better.

The perfectionism illusion is built even further in the age of social media as people post highlight reels of their lives as a way to try and market themselves as having "the good life." Many different influential marketers on social media have cultivated a presence that makes it appear like they never experience reality, but instead, they always experience a carefully crafted existence of perfection every single day. For those who find themselves continually attempting to outperform themselves as a result of perfectionism, they may find themselves attempting to replicate those highlight reels in their everyday life. As a result, they hold themselves to standards that even their role models do not hold themselves to which leads to a chronic cycle of attempting to achieve the unachievable.

The reality is, perfect is an unachievable quality that is virtually pointless to attempt to achieve. Even attempting to achieve close to perfect every single time is not ideal as it can lead to you trying to expect far too much out of yourself on a consistent basis. This does not mean that you shouldn't set your goals high or challenge yourself to do better, but it does mean that you should avoid trying to set your goals so high that they are truly unachievable. Achieving near-perfect results from time to time is reasonable and should be celebrated, but setting the expectation that you will achieve near-perfect results every time will only leave you feeling as badly as true perfectionism will.

By breaking down the myth that you have to be perfect or near-perfect at everything that you do, you give yourself the opportunity to start doing your best. You may have heard a teacher, parent, or friend's parent say this to you at some point in your childhood, "Just try your best." That is because, at the end of the day, your best truly is what matters the most as your best proves that you are challenging yourself and working as hard as you reasonably can towards doing better every time. Even minimal improvements are still something that you can celebrate in your life. You do not have to be perfect at everything or even anything in order to be accepted as a positive and worthy human. You simply have to try your best.

## Allowing yourself to be Imperfect

For someone who struggles with perfectionism, you may find yourself listening the previous section while mentally disagreeing with it or attempting to justify why *your* perfectionism is different. You may attempt to barter with yourself that you are not like other people or that attempting to achieve anything less than perfect is lazy, weak, or pointless. I want you to stop right now and recognize that these very thoughts are not helpful and they will not support you in achieving self-acceptance and self-compassion. The more you attempt to justify why you are the special person that gets to be perfect while everyone else is just human, the longer you are going to hold yourself to unreasonable standards and stay trapped in a constant loop of self-disappointment.

Being imperfect does not mean that you are not going to try your best, achieve great results, or strive for excellence. It simply means that you are not going to criticize yourself to the point of self-sabotage anytime you attempt something in your life and do not achieve perfect results. When you allow yourself to be imperfect, you open yourself up to the capacity to start trying new things because you become willing to embrace the stage of being a beginner who is inexperienced. You trust that not knowing everything is okay because it simply means that you have more to learn and you trust that you have what it takes to learn *in a reasonable amount of time*. Because you have waived the pressure of being an expert on a new subject right off the bat, you give yourself the opportunity to open up to your growth mindset or the mindset of learning. Through this mindset, you equip yourself with the capacity to learn more than ever before, thus taking you directly towards the very same goal that you were so desperately attempting to achieve with perfectionism.

Unfortunately, allowing yourself to be imperfect is not always as simple as making a choice and allowing your life to transform right before your very eyes. Chances are, you are going to experience many moments of setbacks following your decision to become more accepting of who you are. You may find yourself habitually avoiding things in your life because of your fear of not doing them perfectly or you agree to do them only to find yourself fighting to achieve perfection along the way. Having these experiences is completely normal and they actually provide you with an excellent opportunity to begin practicing self-acceptance right away. You can begin by accepting the fact that you are a healing perfectionist and that you are working towards improving your habits so that you can be more self-accepting, but in the meantime, that means embracing where you are at and consciously changing. As you begin to become aware of these moments or setbacks, start by saying "I accept that I have this habit and I am consciously choosing to start changing it right now. I accept that my best is my best and I am willing to be okay with that being the best that I can offer for this." By saying something like this to yourself, you begin to accept where you are at while still aspiring to make changes and consciously choosing to do so. Remember, you cannot be perfect at breaking your perfectionism. It simply does not work like that. It is going to take time, patience, and practice as you begin to reinforce your new habit of being self-accepting no matter what your best looks like.

## Making Peace with Your Past

Part of becoming more self-accepting is being willing to make peace with your past and the way that you behaved or the experiences that you had. You learned about the self and identity in Chapter 1 and now is a great time to recall the auditory self and your experiential self. Chances are the way you experience the world around you and what you are telling yourself through your inner narrator are still heavily linked to past experiences that you have had. Your perception around who you are is likely heavily shaped based on a few highlights in your past, whether they are positive or negative which means that you are probably viewing yourself in a heavily outdated and unrealistic manner.

For many people, their perception of themselves revolves largely around some of their worst experiences in the past. For example, if you were mean towards someone in your past and said something unkind out of a fit of anger and afterward you felt intense guilt around that experience, you may perceive yourself as being unkind, reactive, and mean. This could lead to you believing that you are not worthy of having nice things or being surrounded by nice people because you are too mean and therefore you are undeserving. In reality, you have probably been incredibly nice to many people throughout your life but this is the one thing that continues to play through in your mind and delude you to believing that you are not a good person. If you truly want to move forward and experience a greater sense of self-compassion and self-acceptance, you need to be willing to come to peace with these types of experiences in your life.

You need to develop a sense of trust that who you were is not who you are and that the actions you made no matter how positive or negative they may have been, do not define who you are today. In fact, they have likely never defined who you were, to begin with. Coming to terms with who you were and what you did and accepting that these are all a part of your past allows you to begin accepting yourself and the choices you have made throughout your life. When you begin to accept yourself and your choices, it becomes easier for you to decide to be okay with who you are and okay with what you have done and experienced in your life. That feeling of being okay with your past does not have to mean that you are proud of what you did or that you believe that you have to hold yourself up to the same incredibly high standards as you used to. It simply means that you are willing to accept who you were then just as much as you are willing to accept who you are now which allows you to move forward more gracefully.

If accepting your past is particularly challenging for you, you may choose to move through it at a slower and more intentional pace. Allowing yourself to become okay with just a few things at a time, based on what is relevant to your current life, and moving deeper from there as you go along may be more achievable than attempting to become okay with everything at once. In many cases, your unwillingness to accept your past will arise from a result of you still carrying unexpressed emotions around those experiences. By going through them slowly and with greater intention, you can ensure that you are giving yourself plenty of time and self-compassion to completely feel your way through each memory and move forward more completely as well.

## Revisiting Bad Memories and Difficult Emotions

As you move through the process of accepting your past, there is a good chance that you are going to come across many bad memories and difficult emotions. When you arrive at these bad memories or these difficult emotions arise, you may feel an instinctive desire to shut down or avoid working through these memories so as to avoid being overcome by difficult emotions. In some cases, the pain may be too much to bear. In these circumstances, self-compassion becomes even more crucial as you need to be willing to show compassion towards yourself for the emotions that you are feeling towards these challenging memories.

Throughout the process of revisiting bad memories, it is imperative that you refrain from putting too much pressure on yourself to feel better or heal. Trust that by feeling your emotions and by having compassion for yourself, healing is happening and simply be willing to sit with yourself throughout the process. Do not put an expiration date on your feelings or put a deadline on when you want to be healed by. Just sit with yourself and be willing to slowly navigate through the healing as it happens. When you stop putting so much pressure on being healed and you start sitting with yourself as you revisit painful memories and emotions, healing happens naturally. It does not need to be pushed, forced, or sped up, it simply needs to be honored and experienced.
If you have been sitting with the pain for a while and you find that it is particularly challenging for you to sit with, you might consider moving through it more slowly. Rather than attempting to heal in one afternoon, simply allow yourself to recognize the pain and sit with it for as long as you need to before moving back into your daily living. Revisit that same memory and pain as much as you need to in order to heal it and give yourself as much time in between as you need to in order to become okay with the feelings that you have already felt along

the way. By balancing the process of healing with the process of living, you ensure that you are able to continue living your day to day life while also healing the painful memories that you feel burdened by. Believe it or not, the more you are open to sitting with those challenging emotions as they come, the sooner you feel your way through them and the easier it is for you to get back to your day. Attempting to hide them, repress them, push through them faster to get them out of the way or otherwise become too controlling over your expression of your emotions will only result in them lasting longer. When you feel them as deeply and intensely as you need to, then they begin to move out faster and you are able to move on sooner.

The one thing you do need to be cautious about when it comes to challenging emotions is the unsafe expression. As you feel through your emotions, seek to do so in a safe and constructive manner. If you struggle with handling your emotions and find yourself becoming reactive or dangerous towards yourself or anyone else, it may be best to seek professional support in navigating these emotions. That way, you can release them without doing harm onto yourself or anyone else along the way.

## Finding the Silver Lining of Your Past

As humans, we possess what is known as a "negativity bias" which results in us primarily focusing on the negative. This is our biological way of being able to recall bad experiences so that we could avoid experiencing them again, but it is not always effective particularly when it is unbalanced or not met with positivity. You need to learn how to balance out your mind so that you can focus on your past in a more balanced and realistic manner to avoid feeling as though your life has been one major negative experience.

The best way to begin seeing your past in a more positive light is to start by journaling all of the great things that happened to you. You should start by writing down all of the bad stories you are telling yourself and looking for the silver lining in those bad stories. For example, maybe your parents were not active in your life but you had a grandparent or an aunt or uncle who was. Maybe you got divorced when you were younger and it was particularly painful, but the beginning of the relationship was magical and magnetic. Maybe you got bullied a lot in school, but being bullied lead to you finding your best friend and to this day you two still remain close friends.

By identifying what negative stories you are telling yourself and choosing to see them as having a silver lining, you do not erase the fact that they are painful or those bad things happened. You simply choose to recognize that it wasn't *all* bad and that you did have many positive experiences throughout your life. When you start to create this sort of mental balance between the good things and the bad things that happened in your life, it becomes easier for you to see that there have been many positive elements to your existence. Accepting your past becomes a lot easier because you realize that, although it may contain a lot of pain, it also contains a lot of happiness.

## Accepting Your Past and Moving On

After you have chosen to accept your past and you have decided that you are ready to begin moving forward, it is up to you to decide what that is going to look like. Until now, chances are, you have been carrying on with your life as though you are being held captive by your past choices and mistakes. This means that, in choosing to heal and accept those past choices and mistakes, you also need to choose what it is going to look like for you to move forward. In order for you to do so, you need to have positive forward-focused goals that are going to allow you to relieve yourself of the habits you carry from your unhealed self. These goals can be anything from choosing to see more positivity in your life to choosing to complain less when troubling experiences happen. You want to choose your goals based on what feels right for you and what will reflect the most positive change from your healing in a realistic manner.

When you are choosing to accept your past and move on, a great practice for you to do is to choose to wake up every single morning and forgive yourself for everything you have done in your life that has made you upset or ashamed. By forgiving yourself consciously every single day, you remember to stop holding yourself hostage for the mistakes that you have made and the way that these mistakes have impacted you. You also choose to start seeing yourself as a human who is deserving of compassion and second chances, even if you have made countless mistakes in your past.

If forgiving yourself feels challenging, start small and consider using a journal to track your forgiveness. You can easily write down what you are choosing to forgive and how that feels for you to consider forgiveness around the said topic. Be extremely honest with yourself about the feelings you have around the incident you are seeking to forgive and the blockages that have prevented you from forgiving yourself sooner. As you write these things down, the process of bringing them to your awareness and seeing them on paper will help you begin to cultivate a higher level of compassion towards yourself because you will begin to see yourself as a human with feelings. If experiencing compassion towards yourself continues to be challenging, consider how you might feel towards another person if they were to confide in you about all of the things you have just written down. Chances are, if it was coming from someone else, you would feel a lot more compassionate towards them than you may be feeling towards yourself around this very same subject. Use this understanding to begin developing compassion for yourself and to realize that you also deserve compassion for the troubles you have had in your life because you too are human.

It is critical that you realize that the process of getting to forgiveness and moving on is one that requires patience and acceptance in and of itself. Yes, the rewards of your patience and acceptance will be huge, but you will never achieve them if you do not begin practicing them right away, even if you feel as though you are not ready or worthy enough. The longer you hold onto these fallacies, the harder it is going to be for you to move forward because you will never give yourself the compassion and forgiveness that you need in order to do so. In the beginning, forgiveness may just feel like a subtle shift as you move forward in your life, but over time it will become easier and it will integrate more deeply with your begin. Forgiveness is a process and finding the capacity to begin forgiving yourself is equally as important as finding the capacity to forgive fully.

As forgiving yourself becomes easier and the forgiveness begins to sink in, living your life day in and day out becomes simpler because you are no longer living as a victim of your past. Instead, you begin to fully accept and integrate your past and let yourself off of the hook for troubling mistakes you have made along the way. As you do, leading your life from a clearer and more compassionate frame of mind becomes more achievable and thus your entire life improves because you are leading with your best foot forward.

## Accepting Your Shortcomings

Every single human is born with their own perceived set of flaws that they must learn to come to terms with and accept as a part of who they are. From bodily imperfections to emotional or cognitive imperfections, every single person has something that they believe in some way makes them abnormal compared to everyone else. Even the people who seem to have it all or who behave in a way that leads you to believe that they have no flaws or difficulties are people who struggle with imperfections or who have put in a lot of time to accept themselves as they are. Not one person exists on this planet who has not had to overcome the feeling of having imperfections that result in them feeling like they are undeserving of love or goodness or like they are not valuable or worthy. Again, living in a world where social media is as largely praised as it is and people share only their highlight reels, comparing yourself to others and magnifying the intensity of your perceived flaws becomes even more dangerous. So many people believe that they are unworthy or undeserving because they look outside and only see the best in others, yet only see the worst in themselves. I am willing to bet that you have been guilty of doing this very thing in your own life too because no one is immune to this self-sabotaging behavior.

As you grow older and live with your flaws longer, you have two choices — to continue hating them and hiding for fear of being "found out" or to accept them as they are and proceed with your life anyway. If you choose the former, you will only be holding yourself back as chances are no one who truly means anything to your life or to your success will care about your flaws. If you choose the latter, you put the power of your future into your own hands and enable yourself to design your life in any way you want, regardless of what your flaws may look like or how they may impact you. People who are willing to embrace their flaws and accept them as they are, become people who are willing to grow through their challenges and overcome any obstacle that may be set in their path.

Growing accepting over your flaws whether they are physical or hidden in the inner world takes time and practice. You need to be willing to put forth an accepting and patient hand that lends you the support you need to move forward and overcomes your fears of what might happen if people "found out" about your flaws. You quite literally need to be willing to be the person who will lift yourself up so that when you reach the other side of acceptance, it is you who accept yourself and not someone else that you have become dependent on for acceptance. As you can probably imagine, this requires a lot of self-awareness, self-compassion, self-acceptance, and a willingness to be gentle with yourself as you figure out the process and find your way to success.

How you find your own self-compassion and self-acceptance will depend on what your present feelings towards yourself are and how willing to be compassionate towards yourself you are. If you are listening this audiobook, I would imagine that you likely have a great desire to be compassionate towards yourself but realize this — desire does not equal willingness. You need to truly be willing to be unconditionally compassionate and accepting of yourself if you are ever going to make a change in your life or else changes will never truly stick with you.

Some practices you can try include getting realistic with yourself and checking your perception to make sure that you are being honest in your inner communications. For example, if you are continually telling yourself that you are ugly because you have a birthmark on your face, stop and truly consider whether this is true or not. You may not like the appearance of the birthmark, but is that because you have been taught not to love it or because you genuinely do not love it? Is your lack of love towards your perceived flaw because you have been bullied into believing that it made you unworthy, or because someone meaningful to you told you that you would be much more attractive without it? Do you genuinely believe that your birthmark or any other flaw you may possess is the real reason that you are not receiving all that you desire in life? Or is it because you are allowing it to hold you back due to a fear of being seen and truly receiving what you want from life? Maybe the problem is not your flaw, but your fear of what it might take for you to get what you desire and so you use your flaw as an excuse to hold you back.

Think about it, you were not born as a perfect human— you were born as a real human. You were born as a complete person with likes and dislikes, strengths and weaknesses, and various differences that would grow to exist between yourself and the rest of the world. All of us were born this way. Just because you are unique does not necessarily mean that you are quite as different as you may believe you are. It simply means that you are a real human just like the rest of us. Although there may be things that are different about you, there are things that are different about everyone else too. This is something we all share in common. So you see, even though it sounds unlikely, your differences actually make you pretty normal and you deserve to allow yourself to behave in whatever way feels normal to you without having to dance around your perceived flaws along the way. You can safely embrace the fullness of who you are and trust that no matter how bad they may seem, your flaws are never bad enough to result in you being unworthy of anything that life has to offer you.

## Accepting Your Future Self

Believe it or not, there is a deep need for you to accept your future self just as much as you need to accept yourself as you are and accept your past as it was. If you don't, you may end up holding your future self to the same unreasonably high standards that you have just let your present and past self off of the hook for. This often happens when you heal your present and past self but fail to analyze your goals and make sure that you are being reasonable towards your future self, too. If you continue holding yourself up to goals that are beyond reasonable or dreams that are unachievable, you are only going to set yourself up for failure when you never achieve them.

Now, I'm not saying that your dreams or goals should not be challenging or that anything you truly desire to have is not achievable. After all, airplanes and hovercrafts exist, don't they? Humans really can do anything that they put their mind towards, so technically there is almost nothing that we cannot accomplish as a society or even as individual people. However, people who set big dreams and goals also realize that there is always the chance that their outcome may not look exactly as they had desired for it to look. They may discover instead that all of their efforts ended up leading them down a different path or towards a different future than they had envisioned all along. When this happens, that person can choose to feel like a constant failure because they never achieved the original dream or they can feel grateful to the original dream for giving them the encouragement that they needed to achieve their present success.

See, life will never go the way you plan for it to go, no matter how hard you attempt to stay on track with that plan. You will continually learn new things and discover new information that helps you evolve and grow as a person which means that what you are working towards will evolve and grow too. For example, say you went to school to become a behavioral psychologist and you found that you had a particular attraction towards neuroscience and the brain to the point that you preferred it over your original study of behavioral psychology. Although you may have entered school with the dream of becoming a behavioral psychologist, your introduction to the brain and its functions through those psychology classes resulted in you to realize that you were more passionate about the brain. So, if you were to go ahead and pursue neuroscience and become a brain surgeon, would that make you any less successful? No. It would simply mean that your original plan was changed by the evolution of your life and the unfolding of natural events. If you do not consciously let your future self off of the hook, you may find yourself becoming hung up on the fact that you can never see things through or that you struggle to make up your mind, rather than proud of the fact that you are a brain surgeon.

This is not restricted to large events either which may be easier for you to justify over smaller things that had seemingly less obvious or valuable outcomes than the larger shifts in your life. However, it is imperative that you realize that even the smaller evolutions matter as they are all designed to help you continue moving down a path of life that you genuinely love and that bring you sincere joy and happiness. If you do not let your future self off of the hook for changing your mind and evolving naturally, you may simply find every reason to criticize yourself for changing your mind, even though changing your mind may have been exactly the right thing to do.

A practice regularly used when it comes to accepting your future self in advance is called "releasing the outcome." In other words, you focus on setting the intention for what you desire in your life and you release the outcome by agreeing that if things work out differently than if you had planned, you will still be just as grateful and happy for your success. When you release the outcome, you are not saying that the outcome does not exist or that it is not worthy of pursuing. Instead, you are simply using your present dream and goal as your motivation to move forward and accept that it will change along the way. In this case, your dream or goal becomes a tool to help you continue moving forward and not a finite end result that allows you to determine whether or not you have been successful in your life.

# Chapter 4: Silence and Self-Criticism

Most people are fairly unaware of the power that their inner critic has and how drastically it impacts their life. Many believe that the voice of their inner critic or their autobiographical self is finite and true and that everything it says is to be believed and accepted as the ultimate truth. Of course, this is not the case but we are seldom taught to see our inner critic as an untrained inner voice that truly believes it is trying to help us yet has no idea that it is going about it in the wrong way. Think of your inner critic as your overly blunt best friend — they believe they are telling you what you need to hear so that you can do better but in reality, what they say may hurt and result in you feeling unworthy and incapable. In other words, their intentions may be great but their execution is terrible which means that their approach needs to be adjusted. Just like you would with an overly blunt best friend, you need to confront your inner critic and teach it how to start treating you in a more polite and effective manner.

When you learn to master your inner critic and use it to your advantage rather than allowing it to tear you down, your inner critic becomes a powerful tool that you can enjoy in your life. Instead of holding you back or leading to your self-sabotaging behaviors, it starts propelling you forward through life and giving you the support that you need to succeed. Mastering your inner critic can also help you begin enjoying silence in your life more, as you will not spend every moment of silence being filled with the harsh echoes of your inner critic. Instead, your moments of silence will be genuinely peaceful and enjoyable and will support you in feeling even better in your life.

## Turning Self-Criticism into a Gentle Supporter

Unrelenting self-criticism can be damaging and painful to endure, but not all forms of self-criticism need to be unrelenting and unmanageable. In fact, if you learn how to master your inner critic, it can become one of the gentlest yet effective supports you have in your life. The key is to discover how self-criticism truly can be mastered so that your inner critic is not running rampant and spewing hurtful criticism in your direction at any given moment. Instead, the gentle self-critic is a voice that recognizes opportunities to improve and provides you with self-awareness and understanding that allows you to begin growing in a positive manner, rather than feeling battered by your inner self. As with anything, learning how to embrace your inner self-critic and master it in a way that allows it to become gentle and supportive takes time, patience, and practice.

One way that you can begin to turn your inner self-critic into a gentle supporter is by teaching yourself to criticize behaviors instead of attributes. Unlike attributes, behavior can be changed and improved upon which means that if you are criticizing these, there is actually something that you can do about it to make things better. If you spend all of your time criticizing your attributes, you will always feel like there is nothing that you can do to have a better life because you will always be judging yourself based on things you cannot change. Learning to accept the things that you cannot change and critique and improve on the things that you can is a critical balance that is going to allow you to improve your life in massive ways.

When you are critiquing your behaviors, seek to do so in a way that is productive and effective. Realize that there is a difference between bullying yourself over a mistake and recognizing a mistake and looking for opportunities to improve upon it. If you bully yourself, you are always going to feel as though you are unable to make changes in your life because there is something inherently wrong with you or your previous mistakes mean that you are not deserving of a positive future. This is not constructive in helping you move forward and live a better life. It will only hold you back further. You need to have compassion towards yourself and offer yourself criticism in a way that allows you to actually act upon it and make changes in your life. Seek to empower yourself by pointing out your faults and offering a word of advice, rather than attempting to whip yourself into submission.

A powerful way to confront your inner critic and choose to share in a more compassionate and meaningful way is to look in the mirror and confront your inner critic and all that it has said to you. Recognize that it has always attempted to lead you down the right path and thank it for that, then get clear with yourself about how the criticizing truly feels. Do not be afraid to be honest about how it makes you feel regardless of how painful it may be to admit these feelings to yourself. Speak to your inner critic as if it were another person and be completely clear about how you feel and what you need. When you address yourself in this manner, recognizing your feelings and how damaging your current processes are becomes a lot easier because you bring the emotions and thoughts to light rather than attempting to repress them.

Going forward, each time you hear your inner critic growing harsh and abusive, slow down and remind yourself to approach your need for change in a more compassionate and mindful manner. Take the time to honestly address your feelings and what you believe you need to improve on and then make the conscious effort to begin improving upon those things. Each time you find yourself engaging in your old habit of being mean towards yourself, forgive yourself for that experience and consciously switch the vocabulary so that the criticism comes across more meaningful and polite. For example, say you feel that you struggle to communicate with others and you regularly find yourself wishing that you could share more meaningful and effective conversations with those around you. If your inner critic is unrelenting, it may begin to say things like "I am horrible at communication, I can never say the right things. I can't believe I said that. I must have sounded so stupid. I am so embarrassed about this I should not engage in conversations like this anymore. Clearly, I am incapable." This type of inner dialogue is common but as you can probably see just by reading those words off of the paper, it is mean and hurtful. If you regularly think these things, you will always think that you are incapable and that you must avoid situations where your inabilities shine through such as conversations in this situation. Naturally, conversations are unavoidable so every time you engage in one and these thoughts arise, you will only use it as further evidence that you are unworthy and incapable.

Instead, you could change the dialogue to say something more polite such as "I tried my best, but I definitely think I could have done better. When I said that, I should have been more clear and confident about what I was saying so that I was taken more seriously. I will do better next time so that I can improve on my speaking abilities and have better conversations." Not only is that a significantly more polite way of approaching yourself when it comes to criticism, but it is also done in a way that is actually constructive and supportive. When you give yourself criticism in this way, you reflect on what you felt went wrong and search for a solution immediately so that you can improve in the future. That way, you do not feel as though you are at the mercy of your inabilities because you are clearly focusing on doing better.

## Activating Your Growth Mindset

Having a growth mindset means that your focus is always on looking for ways that you can improve yourself and your life. Rather than consistently staying focused on your flaws and setbacks, you focus on the things that you truly can control and then you put in every effort to improve those things. Some people naturally foster a growth mindset over the course of their lives whereas other people have to consciously focus on developing a growth mindset later in life. If you are looking to activate your growth mindset so that you can have more compassion for yourself and focus more deeply on where you can improve your life rather than obsessing over your flaws, the following strategies will help you.

### *View Your Challenges as Opportunities*

A major component of the growth mindset is switching how you view challenges in your life. When you choose to see your challenges as a way for you to improve or move forward in your life, you literally open your mind up to a whole new world of opportunities. Rather than using excuses, victimizing yourself, or complaining every time you see a challenge arise in your life, choose to see it as an opportunity instead. Viewing your challenges as opportunities means that you take away their power to hold you back and prevent you from growing.

Each time you face a new challenge in your life, refrain from asking yourself "why is this happening to me?" and start asking yourself "what is this teaching me?" When you make this simple change in your perspective, seeing the opportunities that each obstacle presents becomes easier and you realize that you have far more options than simple defeat.

## *Try Learning in New Ways*

There are actually four different ways of learning new information —
visual, auditory, verbal, and physical. Some people need to see things
in clear detail in order to understand them, whereas other people need
to physically practice what they are being taught in order to make
sense of the information. Everyone can learn in each of these ways but
people tend to be more effective at learning in one style over the others.
By discovering what learning style serves you best, you can ensure
that you always tailor your learning to that style as much as you can.
That way, you are far more likely to absorb what you are learning and
genuinely improve your skills rather than feel defeated or like you are
incapable of learning the information at hand.

## *Say "Learning" Instead of "Failing"*

Just like you want to reframe your challenges as being opportunities,
you also want to reframe your failures as lessons. When you say that
something is a failure, you view it as being finite and finished, thus
leading you to behave like there is no alternative to the outcome that
you have received. People who believe in failure find themselves
feeling as though they are always being trampled on by life and like
they have no solutions to move forward and create the life that they
deserve. They frequently take advantage of excuses as a way to avoid
having to try again and often these people genuinely believe that their
excuses provide a genuine reason as to why they cannot proceed.

If you want to find yourself regularly being held down by your
setbacks and seeing every lesson as a failure, you are going to find
yourself offering every excuse under the sun for why you cannot try
again. In the end, you will only be robbing yourself of growth potential
and preventing yourself from achieving the success that you desire.
You need to reframe your failure so that you can begin seeing it as an
opportunity to continue learning, rather than a finite ending to
something that you deeply desire. You are not unable to move beyond
failure and learn from it, you simply need to reframe how you perceive
failure so that you can grow past it every single time.

## Value the Process More

When you value the outcome, you end up slacking or cutting corners during the process so that you can achieve the success that you desire. What ends up happening is that your success is unsustainable because it is based on things that you do not truly know or understand. Thus, when something inevitably shakes it and you are put in a position where you need to perform, you are unable to perform effectively and everything falls apart. No one wins when you slack on the learning process and jump straight to the outcome.

Furthermore, as you already know, the outcome rarely looks the way you believe it will. If you favor the outcome more than the process, you will completely lose the joy and value in the process because you will be so fixated on what results you were planning on getting out of it. Take your time and invest in the day to day learning, it will serve you a lot more when it comes to finding value in your life and gaining genuine skills that will sustain you for the long haul.

## Celebrate Your Growth with Others

Attempting to celebrate your growth on your own can become extremely lonely and fast. When it feels like you are the only one who cares about your growth and success, sometimes it can feel mildly pointless and like it may not be worth it for you to continue pursuing. That doesn't mean that you should make your growth all about receiving positive attention from other people, but inviting other people to celebrate in your growth can make it feel more meaningful and real.

When you take big steps towards celebrating new growth in your life, do not be afraid to invite those who care about you to celebrate your growth with you. Instead of holing up in your house watching a good movie by yourself, invite a good friend or even several good friends out to dinner with you. Celebrate your growth by spending time with the people that you care about and making it truly meaningful as this feels far more rewarding and special than celebrating it alone every single time.

## Reward Your Actions Not Your Traits

A major drawback of living in the age of social media is that we have a tendency to see other people's traits and not necessarily their actions or behaviors. What can end up happening is that you find yourself only acknowledging your own traits and comparing them against others as well. Remember, traits or attributes are not things that you can change about yourself — they simply exist as they are.

If you want to really activate your growth mindset, focus on your behaviors and actions and reward yourself for positive behaviors. This will make it easier for you to start focusing on the parts of yourself that you can change and that when changed, can have a tremendously positive impact on your personal growth.

## Care about Effort over Talent

Putting too much emphasis on your talents or the talents of others can leave you feeling incredibly judgmental over trivial things. Talent can be cultivated, meaning that anyone can become talented at anything as long as they put their mind to it and truly keep trying. This means that it is not the current level of talent that truly matters, but instead, it is the current level of effort that truly matters. People who are bound for success are going to be focusing on their efforts and putting a large amount of energy into achieving positive results from their efforts. As a result, they are more likely to succeed.

This is also a great tool to use if you are recovering from perfectionism and are working towards releasing yourself from having to get everything right from the start. When you begin to care about your own efforts more than your current level of talent, you begin to open up the energy that you need in order to achieve your desired success without putting so much pressure on yourself for not being the best right away. People who do end up achieving statuses like "the best" do not get there from trying to be perfect right away. They get there from constant, intentional effort.

*Take Responsibility for Yourself*

You are the only person who is responsible for everything that you have done in your life, not anyone else. Although other people may have contributed to your decisions, at the end of the day, they were not the ones who made those decisions for you, you made them. You need to realize that you are the only one who can take responsibility for yourself. When you do, making the decision to behave in a way that allows you to step out of victim mentality and into the mindset that is required for continuous growth becomes significantly easier.

Starting today, work towards taking responsibility for every single action and decision that you make. Do not let anyone else pressure you into choosing decisions that you did not truly want to make or taking actions that you truly did not want to take. When you take responsibility, you will find that it is much easier for you to then choose to take the actions that *you* want to take such as growing and improving upon yourself.

## Dealing With Your Mistakes

Everyone makes mistakes. That is just a fact of life. You may have heard the saying before that goes "It doesn't matter what mistakes you make in life, what does matter is how you proceed after making those mistakes." If you make a mistake and you continually make the same mistake repeatedly, then you can guarantee that you are not actively or effectively learning the lessons that you need to in order to generate success in your life. Instead, you are staying trapped in habits and cycles that are preventing you from growing because you refuse to recognize your mistakes and make new decisions. Once again, this is another example of where taking responsibility for yourself and your life becomes valuable. When you take responsibility, you commit to taking the actions required to make a change.

Anytime you make a mistake in your life and find yourself facing results that you do not desire, commit to learning how you can move beyond those mistakes and start generating more positive results from your efforts. As you do, you will begin to find ways that you can learn and grow from your mistakes so that you do not find yourself consistently making the same ones over and over again. You can commit to finding the solution by getting yourself focused on discovering where your efforts went wrong and how you might have handled the situation differently. This allows you to dissect the mistake and see what went right and what didn't, which ensures that you are actually correcting the proper problematic behavior.

After you have discovered where the problematic behavior or action lies, you can start looking for honest solutions that allow you to improve going forward so that you do not repeatedly make the same mistakes time and again. When you give this amount of attention to improving yourself, what ends up happening is that not only do you achieve personal growth but you also achieve personal pride. Rather than feeling embarrassed, frustrated, or defeated by being trapped inside of a habit loop or a behavioral pattern, you can feel confident in your consistent improvements. This gives yourself a sense of hope that you are going to continue doing and achieving better things in life, while also allowing you to remain compassionate towards yourself when your efforts do not pay off immediately. Because you can trust in your own problem-solving abilities and your deep inner desire to change, you can trust that you are not always going to be stuck experiencing the same unwanted situations over and over again.

Aside from looking for your opportunity to improve upon your previous mistakes and making a plan to do so, you should also spend some time forgiving yourself when you have made a mistake in your life. Failure to genuinely forgive yourself can leave you feeling unresolved emotions that can result in you generating deep seeded resentment or mistrust towards yourself. Take the time to address your emotions and feel your way through the situation while also logically planning your next steps so that you can fully complete the cycle of the mistake and start stepping away from it more productively going forward.

## Moving on after You've Made an Error

After you have made an error in your life, knowing how to completely move on is imperative. As you know, forgiving yourself and making a plan are two important components of moving forward because this allows you to complete the cycle and feel confident that your solution is effective enough to help you do better next time. There are other things that you should do when you are moving on from an error to help you feel a more complete sense of moving on as well, however.

One thing that you should do is communicate with anyone else who may have been affected by your error to ensure that your intentions and feelings are made clear. This also gives you the opportunity to apologize if an apology is needed which ensures that nothing is left unfinished. If you do not take the time to communicate with others and bring closure to a situation that involves other people, it can generate feelings of resentment, mistrust, and guilt. You may find that the other person struggles to trust you because you were unable to admit to your mistake and that you feel a tremendous amount of guilt around making the said mistake that leaves you embarrassed or afraid of approaching them. This can destroy relationships so bringing in an element of communication and healing any relationships that may have been damaged in the process is important. Doing so will ensure that being compassionate towards yourself is easier because you know that you did everything you could to make the situation better and you were not left feeling guilty or blaming yourself for not apologizing or correcting the situation sooner.

The next thing that you need to do is bring in an element of gratitude so that you can begin seeing the positive in your mistake. For some mistakes, seeing the positive element is going to be challenging because the mistake may have been so large and impactful that you genuinely feel as though nothing good could have possibly come from it. In these situations, look for the things that you have learned following the mistake and see how that mistake has changed your life since happening. These are all things that you can be grateful for even if the mistake itself feels like something so bad that nothing good could possibly come from it.

Anytime you make a mistake in your life, always look to see how it has changed you and how you have grown since the mistake was made. This will help you really begin adopting the growth mindset mentality of nothing being a failure because everything you endure is a lesson. When you are able to embody that mentality and begin exercising it in your real life, allowing yourself to truly grow becomes significantly easier.

## Letting Go of Overthinking

The final step to overcoming self-criticism and allowing yourself to move on from mistakes that you have made in your life is to make sure that you let go of over thinking. Overthinking can result in you repeatedly going over the same experience in your head over and over again, analyzing every single aspect of the experience, and trying to find new ways to guard yourself against it. Typically, this behavior is intended to help you completely overcome behaviors that have caused you pain or brought you a discomfort in your life, but in the end, it only makes you feel worse. When you over think things, you tend to put far too much pressure on yourself to completely change your behavior in one go to avoid experiencing the same pain that your original mistake brought you. Unfortunately, no one can change all of their behaviors that quickly which will result in you only feeling worse the next time you make a similar mistake because you will feel as though you already had the perfect solution so it is your fault for performing poorly. In reality, you simply had far too high of expectations on yourself so it was virtually impossible for you to measure up to your unreasonable standards.

Not only does over thinking cause you to set unreasonable standards upon yourself, but it also causes you to spend far more time worrying and feeling bad about yourself than you need to. When you are over thinking, you keep a situation in your head far longer than it deserves to actually be there. If you are an avid overthinker, you may find yourself doing this with many different experiences and subjects which leave you feeling even worse and tremendously overwhelmed. Your brain becomes fixated on all of the ways that you believe you are underperforming in life, which can leave you struggling to find any ways that you are performing positively because you are constantly focused on your negative performance.

Simply giving up on over thinking is not always an option. If you have been over thinking for a long time or if you struggle with something like anxiety, then you may find that giving up on over thinking takes a lot of effort. Fortunately, you now know that your emphasis should be focused on the amount of effort that you have put in and not the number of results that you are getting each time. Staying focused on your efforts will ensure that you are focused on making progress which will help you truly achieve your progress in the long run.

The first step to overcoming overthinking is to start becoming aware of how big of a problem overthinking truly is for you. When you begin to practice self-awareness and become aware over how often you are over thinking and how it is making you feel, it becomes easier for you to be honest with yourself about how often you are over thinking things. Through this honesty, you can get clear and realistic on your expectations for how you can improve and what that improvement will look like over time. This way, you do not accidentally set unrealistic expectations on yourself due to a lack of truly being aware of how much your overthinking is impacting you.

Once you are clear on how much you are over thinking and have generated realistic goals on how you can overcome over thinking, you need to start equipping yourself with the necessary tools to break the habit. One great tool is to start teaching yourself to focus on what could go right rather than staying fixated on what could go wrong. While you do still want to be aware of potential problems you may face, also become aware of what positive outcomes you could experience and how they may impact your life. Becoming realistic about all of the possible outcomes including the positive ones helps you to see that every situation has many positive and negative solutions that can be derived from them. Through this, it becomes easier to stay neutral or hopeful rather than negative and fearful around what undesirable outcomes you may encounter along the way.

Another way to begin overcoming over thinking is to break the cycle through distractions. When you distract yourself into being happier, your brain learns to start breaking down the cycles that lead to overthinking and literally wires itself into having new habits instead. You can easily distract yourself from over thinking through using positive affirmations, enjoyable hobbies or activities, exercise, or trying something new or different from your usual activities. By breaking out of your normal routine or putting your focus on something more productive, your brain is forced to pay attention which results in you no longer overthinking.

Sometimes overthinking stems from not giving yourself enough time to adequately assess each situation that you are entering. If you are someone who regularly jumps into situations without much thought, or if you used to be like that and you have experienced a tremendous number of unwanted outcomes, you may be afraid to take leaps in your current life. As a result, you may rely on things like overthinking to help you avoid making a significant mistake in the future. What ends up happening, however, is that you find yourself trapped in "analysis paralysis" or in a state where you are unable to stay focused or make a move because you are so afraid of failing. In this circumstance, exercising boundaries is imperative as it will support you in having adequate time to assess your situation and make decisions without feeling pressured to act immediately. For over thinking specifically, set a timer for five minutes analyzing everything that you are afraid of and allowing yourself to think through all of the thoughts that are keeping you worried. Then, set it again for ten minutes so that you can write everything down and get it out of your mind, thus preventing you from feeling as though you have to continually think it in order to avoid "forgetting" about your chosen solution. Once you are done journaling, commit to letting go of the situation and move forward using a tool such as distraction to help you fully disengage from your worry and take actionable steps forward.

Lastly, many people will engage in overthinking as a way to make up for what they feel was a poor performance on their behalf. They believe that by over thinking about the situation and identifying every improvement that they could have possibly made then, in some way, they have retroactively improved their performance and made up for their mistakes. In reality, this is not true. No amount of thinking about alternative outcomes will change the way that the situation unfolded. The best thing that you can do is try your best in every single situation and then pick one or two things you might improve on going forward so that you can have a more positive impact. By staying honest with yourself about how much effort you put in and reasonable with yourself about how much you expect to improve going forward, you can break the cycle of chronic over thinking and move forward positively.

# Chapter 5: Mindfulness and Self-Awareness

The final step in fostering a stronger sense of self-compassion is developing your mindfulness and self-awareness. When you develop mindfulness and self-awareness, you equip yourself with the two most important tools required when it comes to improving your relationship with yourself and having a deeper sense of compassion and sympathy towards yourself going forward. People who are more mindful and self-aware have an easier time identifying their self-sabotaging behaviors, putting them into perspective, and moving past them in a productive manner.

In this final chapter, you are going to discover how you can begin building your mindfulness and self-awareness practices in a way that will genuinely support you in feeling a deeper and more meaningful sense of self-compassion. You should seek to implement these practices on a daily basis to ensure that you are always putting in the effort to have a more positive relationship with yourself. As with any relationship in your life, the more genuine attention and care you give to your relationship with yourself, the more you are going to get out of it. Since this is such a personal experience which means that you will experience a greater sense of joy, optimism, self-worth, and self-confidence around your ability to grow and become a better version of yourself every day.

As you go about implementing these practices, remember to embrace deep self-acceptance along the way. Your relationship with yourself may not be where you want it to be right now which may leave you feeling a variety of different emotions such as sadness, pain, anger, and grief. Be patient with these feelings and accept them as they arise so that you can work through them and improve your life going forward.

## Practicing Presence

Presence allows you to become more grounded in your current moment and enjoy it for what it is. When you practice presence, you are able to let go of all of your regrets from the past and all of your worries for the future so that you can enjoy the present moment to the fullest of your ability. Through becoming more centered and present, you give yourself the gift of feeling less mental worry and a greater capacity to genuinely receive moments that bring you joy, happiness, and contentment.

Developing your presence is going to require you to deny everything you have ever learned about the getup and go of modern living and start focusing on how you can start slowing down and really embracing each moment as it comes. Instead of constantly checking your calendar or clock for indication of it being time to move onto the next activity, slow down and allow your self to fully immerse into the current one for as long as it lasts. You can do this by setting regular breaks for yourself and committing to completely releasing any unwanted thoughts from your psyche during those breaks, such as thoughts that have you focusing on what comes next or what needs to get done. Once you have released those thoughts, bask in the silence of the moment and start to become aware of what is going on around you right now in the present moment. As you read this even, slow down and take a break so that you can become present in your experience. Notice what is around you, listen to the sounds going on in your environment, and pay attention to any feelings you may be having right now. Getting actively engaged at the moment brings you out of your thoughts and into the experience so that you can start freeing up mental space and enjoying your life more fully.

If you find that you are the type of person who constantly doubles, triple, and quadruple check your watch or phone for an indication that it is time for you to move on to the next activity, look for a more productive way to manage your time. Rather than constantly feeling a nagging to check the time, set an alarm or a reminder that will go off a few minutes before you need to switch activities. This way, you can completely let go of the need to check the time over and over again and start focusing on being present. Instead of the constant distraction, you can trust that you are going to be informed of your next activity with plenty of time without you having to personally pay attention to the time itself.

Lastly, developing a meditation practice is a great way for you to practice releasing your busy mindset habits and start focusing on the present moment. When you develop a meditation practice you give yourself the opportunity to intentionally slow down and practice presence through your meditation. Research suggests that just 10 minutes of meditating each day, ideally in the morning, will support you in having a greater ability to feel more at peace while also staying more present from moment to moment.

## Feeling Deeply and Moving On Completely

A highly valuable practice you can use to start developing a deeper sense of mindfulness and self-awareness is to start allowing yourself to deeply feel before moving on completely. In many instances, we find ourselves feeling busy, rushed, and disengaged from every situation that we encounter because we are struggling to fully feel every experience that we have in our lives. When you struggle to feel things deeply, your mind attempts to hold on to those memories and emotions so that you can revisit them at a later time. When you never give yourself that later time, you find yourself holding on to too many things inside of you so you struggle to fully sink into each moment and emotion which keeps you in the cycle of never fully feeling and releasing.

In order to help you deepen your presence and have better experiences in life, begin fostering the art of feeling deeply and releasing completely. Each time you engage in a new moment or feel a new emotion arise, allow it to completely wash over you and feel it to the very depths of what it is. This does not necessarily mean that you need to act on every single emotion to the maximum extent that you can. Instead, just focus on acknowledging it and how far it goes and allow it to really sink into your heart and body as a true and genuine emotion that you are experiencing. If you are in a place where it is safe to do so, do not be afraid to let your emotions out completely by crying, yelling, punching a pillow, or simply lying down and feeling the despair wash through you. Once you have completely felt the depths of the emotion, allow it to be released completely. Since you have felt it completely, releasing it completely is easier because there is nothing residing within you that keeps you attached to that emotion.

If you do find that you are somewhere that seems unacceptable for you to release your emotions such as at work or in an important meeting, give yourself permission to file them away for later. When you do, always make sure that you come back to that emotion as soon as it is reasonable for you to do so and feel into it completely so that you can also release it completely. By setting the intention to dig into and feel that emotion all the way, you ensure that it does not fester and result in you experiencing it any more than you need to.

## The Value of Daily Reminders

As you go about changing your habits to incorporate for more mindfulness and self-awareness, nothing will prove to be more valuable than the very simple tool of daily reminders. Having daily reminders in your life to support you in remembering to engage in a mindfulness practice or become aware over your present state of being can support you in actually remembering to engage in and reinforce your new positive habits. The more you see your reminders and engage in your mindfulness and self-awareness, the easier it will be for you to start reminding yourself to engage in these behaviors as well. Over time, you will find that your inner ability to remember and then actually fully engage will improve, allowing you to experience more joy and positivity from your life.

There are many ways that you can set daily reminders for yourself so that you actually pay attention and listen to them. The best way is to set daily reminders in a variety of different ways so that you are actually paying attention and following those reminders as seeing the exact same reminder too often may lead to you ignoring it. You can set reminders on your phone to periodically remind you throughout the day, leave post-it notes around your home and office, and even write it down in your calendar.

Another creative way to remind yourself to engage in mindfulness is to set triggers that are meant to help remind you spontaneously. For example, maybe you decide that from now on every single time you see the color orange you are going to pause for a moment and begin practicing mindfulness and self-awareness. By setting triggers like this, you ensure that you are going to practice mindfulness at all times and not just when you see the reminder on your phone go off or the note in your day timer each morning.

The more reminders you set and the more you commit to actually acting on those reminders, the easier it will be for you to get the fullest value out of them. Over time, you will become so used to these reminders that you will naturally begin engaging in mindfulness and self-awareness all on your own. Any time you notice an intense wave of emotion or a challenging situation surface before you, you will slow down and tap into your mindfulness and self-awareness practices so that you can begin feeling more positive overall. This will continue to develop as you continue to improve your growth mindset which will ultimately lead to you experiencing a continually more positive life experience overall.

## Meditation for Mindfulness and Self-Reflection

There are many meditations that you can practice for mindfulness and self-reflection, including the two following ones that I have provided for you. The first one is a shorter meditation that you can practice on the go any time you find yourself feeling intense emotions or energies rushing through your body and find yourself needing to check in with yourself. The second is longer and gives you a more intentional and meaningful connection with yourself so that you can really tune into your inner feelings and process them more effectively. You should seek to use each of these daily, as they will both provide you with great value in improving your overall mindfulness and self-awareness and help you to feel a deeper sense of peace and calm in your life.

### A Quick Breathing Meditation

In order to practice this quick breathing meditation, you simply need 2-3 minutes of personal time and a willingness to tune in and fully listen during that period of time. Then, all you need to do is sit or stand somewhere that you will not be distracted and straighten out your posture. Focus on elongating your back, dropping your shoulders, letting your tongue muscles relax, relaxing your core, and fully embracing a moment of peace. When you have completely relaxed your body, take a few deep breaths in and out, counting to four with each inhalation and counting to four with each exhalation, aiming to take at least ten complete breaths.

After you have taken your breaths, ask yourself "How am I feeling right now?" and "What do I need right now?" Listen to the answers that arise so that you can get a clear sense of what emotions arise for you and what needs you may have that are not presently being met. Then, completely acknowledge your emotions and your needs and create a plan to feel through your emotions and fulfill your needs as soon as you possibly can. By acknowledging what you are feeling and what you need and creating a plan to address these two things, you assure yourself that there is no need to worry or feel neglected because you are actively seeking to improve your present conditions.

If you are in a moment where you can actively feel through your emotions or meet your needs, do so right away. If you aren't, be very diligent about coming back to your emotions and needs at a later time and fulfilling them completely as this will allow you to begin developing a sense of trust in yourself and your ability to take care of yourself completely.

### *A Full Body Scan Meditation*

The full body scan meditation is one that you should attempt to accomplish on a daily basis. One great body scan every day, ideally at night time, is a great opportunity for you to check in with yourself, get a sense of what is going on within your mind, and tap into any emotions or thoughts that may be unresolved from the previous day. Consider this as your opportunity to show yourself compassion on purpose particularly if you have been having troubles showing compassion for yourself throughout the day. As you begin to give yourself this quality time and pay attention to yourself on a more consistent basis, you will find that you begin cultivating a deeper relationship with yourself that allows you to tune in even more.

To begin your body scan, simply begin by sitting or lying down and taking several deep breaths into your diaphragm. Fill up your lungs as completely as possible, allowing yourself to relax into each breath as you take it for as long as possible. Once you feel yourself entering a state of relaxation, begin drawing your awareness into your body and seeing if you notice any specific areas that are filled with tension. If you do, go through those areas one by one and make a conscious effort to relax them completely before you begin with your official body scan.

With your body completely relaxed, go ahead and draw your consciousness into your feet and take a moment to notice if you are carrying any tension in them before intentionally relaxing them completely. Then, draw your awareness up into your shins and consciously become aware of any tension you may be carrying there and release it completely, too. Continue doing this all the way up your body by drawing your awareness to your knees, thighs, glutes, hips, abdomen and lower back, torso, middle back, chest and upper back, shoulders, biceps, forearms, hands, neck, and head. By consciously drawing awareness into each of your body parts and letting that awareness rise up through you, you give yourself the opportunity to intentionally release any stress that you may be carrying within your body. This is known as a complete body scan or a form of progressive muscle relaxation that allows you to completely de-stress your entire body and release anything that you may be carrying within you. Once you are done, be sure to address any feelings that may have come up along the way and allow yourself to completely process them and then release them so that you are capable of moving forward completely.

## Mindfulness Exercises for You to Try

In addition to meditation, there are many other mindfulness practices that you can try to help you enter a deeper state of mindfulness and self-awareness. These practices range from things that you can actively use to make yourself more consciously aware during your day to day experiences or that you can engage in during your personal time to improve your mindfulness.

### *Spontaneous Environmental Check In*

A spontaneous environmental check-in is a simple practice whereby you slow down and pay attention to the environment around you as you engage in any form of day to day experience. You can do this anytime you notice that you are checking out or struggling to stay grounded in the moment or simply to see just how tuned in you really are. This can be done at work, when you are spending time with friends, or even when you first open your eyes in the morning. The more you practice it, the more mindful you will become.

In order to practice your spontaneous environmental check-in, you simply need to tune into your environment and notice at least one thing that is stimulating each of your senses. So, you want to notice one thing that you see, one thing that you hear, one thing that you feel, one thing that you smell, and one thing that you taste. Since you are likely not tasting your environment at all times, taking a sip of water or chewing a stick of gum is a great way to engage your sense of taste during experiences where you are not actively eating or drinking something as a part of your experience.

### Mindful Listening Practices

Listening is a powerful tool that can help you really plug into your environment. A great listening practice that can be done in your personal time is called mindful listening and it requires you to use a piece of music or composure to help you engage in mindful listening. The goal as you listen to this music is to listen to each word and actively let each word go as you move onto the next word in the song. Rather than attempting to remember what has been said or formulate an opinion or understanding around what the song means, simply listen to it and experience it in complete presence.

### Focusing On Your Details

If you are struggling to stay present or mindful during any particular experience, practice focusing intently on your details. In order to do so, simply bring your awareness into the details of what you are doing. For example, if you are washing dishes, pay attention to the temperature of the water, the texture of the soap, and the visual of watching the dish become clean. Allow yourself to pay close attention to each step of the process and really immerse yourself into how it feels for you so that you can get deeply engaged in the process. By really embracing each detail of the process, you encourage your mind to stay focused on what you are doing rather than allowing it to grow bored and get distracted by other things that may be going on around you.

## Self-Reflection Exercises for You to Try

Self-reflection is a great opportunity for you to improve your self-awareness and develop a deeper understanding around who you are and what you have to offer. Practicing self-reflection on a daily basis gives you the opportunity to both understand yourself on a deeper level and decide what you may wish to improve upon in your life so that you can experience greater results from your self-improvement efforts. You should seek to engage in at least one self-reflection exercise per day so that you can really immerse yourself into your growth and learning, as well as cultivate a strong relationship with yourself.

### *Self-Reflection Journaling*

Nothing beats a good old fashioned journal when it comes to learning how to improve upon yourself and become the best version of yourself that you possibly can. Self-reflection journaling is an easy activity that you can engage in on a daily basis so that you can pay attention to how you are doing and really dig into areas of your life that you want to improve on.
The best way to utilize your self-reflection journal is to write down all of the things that you wish you had done better in your day and all of the things that you are exceptionally proud of. For the things that you wish you had done better, write about why you wish you had done better and how you wish you had done things differently. That way, you have an idea of what you can do in the future as well as a clear understanding as to why it happened so that you can practice true compassion with yourself. For the things that you are proud of, celebrate yourself and take a moment to deeply immerse into your pride around these subjects.

### *Listening In On Your Self-Talk*

Eavesdropping on your self-talk is a great way to listen to how you are communicating with yourself and get a better idea on how you can improve the way that you are speaking to yourself. When you listen in on your self-talk, you can get clear on how it may be helping or hindering your success in life. If your self-talk is compassionate and caring, then chances are you are engaging in positive self-talk that is actually supporting you in moving forward in life. However, if your self-talk sounds harsh or condescending, you can easily regain control over it and move back into a state of deeper compassion so that you are no longer attempting to bully yourself into submission.

## Tracking Your Progress

The best way to track your progress when it comes to personal development, especially around things like mindfulness and self-awareness which tends to be challenging to measure is through snapshot journaling. Snapshot journaling essentially requires you to write one journal entry per week where you get very honest about how you are currently embracing mindfulness and self-awareness in your life. Be very clear about how well you think you are doing and make sure to highlight any areas where you feel that you are not performing as well as you believe you could be.

By honestly capturing how you are feeling in regards to mindfulness and self-awareness or any other aspects of yourself that you are trying to improve on, you give yourself clear progress notes to look back on. You can then read back through your snapshots and see just how much you have changed and how far you have come based on the notes you have taken. Of course, based on the nature of how this works, you will only get incredible results if you stay highly honest with yourself and truly capture the reality of how you are doing each time.

Another way that you can track your progress is to communicate with a loved one who knows you well. By asking for feedback and requesting them to reflect on your growth as far as they have seen, you also give yourself the opportunity to get a clear understanding of your persona and how it may be reflecting your personal improvements. Be sure not to ask too often or it may become overwhelming or ineffective, but do not be afraid to ask from time to time just to get a clear understanding of how far you have come and where you may need to improve on going forward.

# Conclusion

Congratulations on seeing your own personal journey of *Self-Compassion* all the way through until now! While I know your personal journey with cultivating self-compassion will never truly come to an end, our journey together for this audiobook is. Before you go, however, I want to make sure that you truly feel equipped with all of the tools that you need to completely embrace your new skill of self-compassion.

First, I want you to recall the importance of your relationship with yourself and the reality of how your identity is created between three states of awareness that we all possess. I hope that in learning this concept that you were able to develop a stronger understanding of how your perception of who you are and who you truly are will never fully line up. Likewise, how other people see you and who you truly are will never fully line up, either. You are a human with many qualities, characteristics, and aspects to your identity, each of which extends far beyond any one person's perception.

By realizing that your identity is far larger than what you or anyone else thinks of you, I hope you understand how to develop a deeper sense of self-compassion by recognizing that you are not able to be chalked up to any one label. You are by no means incapable, worthless, mean, pathetic, useless, or any other labels that you may be cruelly identifying yourself against. Likewise, you are not any one positive label. In fact, you are many things and in many different ways and who you are change depending on who you are around and what persona you are embracing at that moment. Although there are many constants in who you are, there are also many evolving pieces of your identity that contribute to the reason as to why "who" you are is such a challenging thing to summarize.

When you stop trying to identify yourself as any one thing and you open your mind up to the concept that you are many things and nothing all at the same time, it becomes easier for you to stop attaching yourself to labels. In that, you give yourself the freedom you require to begin developing a deeper and gentler connection with yourself and all aspects of your inner identity. The more you detach from labels and the belief that you are one finite identity, the more you will find yourself feeling the freedom to love yourself deeply and intensely.

The second thing I want you to take away from this audiobook is that your self-compassion is something that will evolve over time so do not worry if you have reached this point and you do not yet feel a deep sense of compassion for yourself. The more you practice the tools that I have provided you with here in this audiobook, the more you are going to feel a deeper sense of compassion towards yourself. At first, that sense of compassion may barely crack through the surface of everything that you are feeling and the shell that you keep yourself protected by. However, the more you practice, the deeper your compassion towards yourself will become and the easier it will be for you to hold space for yourself and accept yourself as you really are.

Always be willing to accept yourself for where you are at in your journey and have faith that you will improve as you move forward. Remember, it is okay not to be okay and it is okay to feel like you are not where you wish you were in life. If you feel frustrated, sad, or defeated because you are not further ahead in life, that is okay. Accept yourself as you are and for the emotions you have around what you are going through each day and through that acceptance, it will feel easier for you to heal and move forward.

Thank you.

CPSIA information can be obtained
at www.ICGtesting.com
Printed in the USA
BVHW041014090720
583345BV00010B/96